The Letter Tt

By Hollie J. Endres

capstone classroom

It can pull **t**acks.

Will it pull **t**eddy bears?

It can pull **t**ools.

Will it pull **T**-shirts?

It can pull **t**rains.

Will it pull
tape measures?

Will it pull **t**wine?